GENESIS: UNDERSTANDING GOD'S GOODNESS

A four-week course to introduce people to
the central truths of the first book of the Bible.

by
Bob Buller

Apply·It·To·Life™

Adult

BIBLE CURRICULUM
from Group

Group
Loveland, Colorado

Apply·It·To·Life™

Adult

BIBLE CURRICULUM

Group

Genesis: Understanding God's Goodness
Copyright © 1996 Group Publishing, Inc.

Credits
Senior Editor: Paul Woods
Creative Products Director: Joani Schultz
Art Directors: Kathy Benson and Lisa Chandler
Cover Designer: Liz Howe
Cover Illustrator: John Chard; Tony Stone Images
Illustrator: Rex Bohn

ISBN 1-55945-517-9

10 9 8 7 6 5 4 3 2 1   05 04 03 02 01 00 99 98 97 96

Printed in the United States of America.

C O N T E N T S

Introduction

WHAT IS APPLY-IT-TO-LIFE™ ADULT BIBLE CURRICULUM?

Apply-It-To-Life™ Adult Bible Curriculum is a series of four-week study courses designed to help you facilitate powerful lessons that will help class members grow in faith. Use this course with
- Sunday school classes,
- home study groups,
- weekday Bible study groups,
- men's Bible studies,
- women's Bible studies, and
- family classes.

The variety of courses gives the adult student a broad coverage of topical, life-related issues and significant biblical topics. In addition, as the name of the series implies, every lesson helps the adult student apply Scripture to his or her life.

Each course in Apply-It-To-Life Adult Bible Curriculum provides four lessons on different aspects of one topic. In each course, you also receive Fellowship and Outreach Specials connected to the month's topic. They provide suggestions for building closer relationships in your class, outreach activities, and even party ideas!

WHAT MAKES APPLY-IT-TO-LIFE™ ADULT BIBLE CURRICULUM UNIQUE?

Teaching as Jesus Taught

Jesus was a master teacher. With Apply-It-To-Life Adult Bible Curriculum, you'll use the same teaching methods and principles that Jesus used:

● **Active Learning.** Think back on an important lesson you've learned in life. Did you learn it from reading about it? from hearing about it? from something you did? Chances are, the most important lessons you've learned came from something you experienced. That's what active learning is—learning by doing. Active learning leads students through activities and experiences that help them understand important principles, messages, and ideas. It's a discovery process that helps people internalize and remember what they learn.

Jesus often used active learning. One of the most vivid examples is his washing of his disciples' feet. In Apply-It-To-Life Adult Bible Curriculum, the teacher might remove his or her shoes and socks, then read aloud the foot-washing passage from John 13, or the teacher might choose to actually wash people's feet. Participants won't soon forget it. Active learning uses simple activities to teach profound lessons.

● **Interactive Learning.** Interactive learning means learning through small-group interaction and discussion. Each person is actively involved in discovering God's truth. Interactive learning puts people in pairs, trios, or foursomes to involve everyone in the learning experience. It takes active learning a step further by having people who have gone through an experience teach others what they've learned.

Jesus often helped cement the learning from an experience by questioning people—sometimes in small groups—about what had happened. He regularly questioned his followers and his opponents, forcing them to think and to discuss among themselves what he was teaching them. After washing his disciples' feet, the first thing Jesus did was ask the disciples if they understood what he had done. After the "foot washing" activity, the teacher might form small groups and have people discuss how they felt when the leader removed his or her shoes and socks. Then group members could compare those feelings and the learning involved to what the disciples must have experienced.

● **Biblical Depth.** Apply-It-To-Life Adult Bible Curriculum recognizes that most people are ready to go below the surface to better understand the deeper truths of the Bible. Therefore, the activities and studies go beyond an "easy answer" approach to Christian education and lead people to grapple with difficult issues from a biblical perspective.

In the Bible Basis, you'll find information that will help you understand the Scriptures you're dealing with. Within the class-time section of the lesson, thought-provoking activities and discussions lead adults to new depths of biblical understanding. Bible Insights within the lesson give pertinent information that will bring the Bible to life for you and your class members. In-class handouts give adults significant Bible information and challenge them to search for and discover biblical truths for themselves. Finally, the "For Even Deeper Discussion" sections provide questions that will lead your class members to new and deeper levels of insight and application.

No one questions the depth of Jesus' teachings or the effectiveness of his teaching methods. This curriculum follows Jesus' example and helps people probe the depths of the Bible in a way no other adult curriculum does.

● **Bible Application.** Jesus didn't stop with helping people understand truth. It wasn't enough that the rich young ruler knew all the right answers. Jesus wanted him to take action on what he knew. In the same way, Apply-It-To-Life Adult Bible Curriculum encourages a response in people's lives. That's why this curriculum is called "Apply-It-To-Life"! Depth of understanding means little if the truths of Scripture don't zing into people's hearts. Each lesson brings home one point and encourages people to consider the changes they might make in response.

● **One Purpose.** In each study, every activity works toward communicating and applying the same point. People may discover other new truths, but the study doesn't load them down with a mass of information. Sometimes less is more. When lessons try to teach too much, they often fail to teach anything. Even Jesus limited his teaching to what he felt people could really learn and apply (John 16:12). Apply-It-To-Life Adult Bible Curriculum makes sure that class members thoroughly understand and apply one point each week.

● **Variety.** Jesus constantly varied his teaching methods. One day he would have a serious discussion with his disciples about who he was, and another day he'd baffle them by turning water into wine. What he didn't do was allow them to become bored with what he had to teach them.

Any kind of study can become less than exciting if the leader and students do everything the same way week after week. Apply-It-To-Life Adult Bible Curriculum varies activities and approaches to keep everyone's interest level high each week. In one class, you might have people in small groups "put themselves in the disciples' sandals" and experience something of the confusion of Jesus' death and resurrection. In another lesson, class members may experience problems in communication and examine how such problems can damage relationships.

● **Relevance.** People today want to know how to live successfully right now. They struggle with living as authentic Christians at work, in the family, and in the community. They want to know how the Bible can help them live faithful lives—how it can help them face the difficulties of living in today's culture. Apply-It-To-Life Adult Bible Curriculum bridges the gap between biblical truth and the "real world" issues of people's lives. Jesus didn't discuss with his followers the eschatological significance of Ezekiel's wheels, and Apply-It-To-Life Bible Curriculum won't either! Courses and studies in this curriculum focus on the real needs of people and help them discover answers in Scripture that will help meet those needs.

● **A Nonthreatening Atmosphere.** In many adult classes, people feel intimidated because they're new Christians or because they don't have the Bible knowledge they think they should have. Jesus sometimes intimidated those who opposed him, but he consistently treated his followers with understanding and respect. We want people in church to experience the same understanding and respect Jesus' followers experienced. With Apply-It-To-Life Adult Bible Curriculum, no one is embarrassed for not knowing or understanding as much as someone else. In fact, the interactive learning process minimizes the differences between those with vast Bible knowledge and those with little Bible knowledge. Lessons often begin with nonthreatening, sharing questions and move slowly toward more depth. Whatever their level of knowledge or commitment, class members will work together to discover biblical truths that can affect their lives.

● **A Group That Cares.** Jesus chose 12 people who learned from him together. That group practically lived together—sharing one another's hurts, joys, and ambitions. Sometimes Jesus divided the 12 into smaller groups and worked with just three or four at a time.

Adults today long for a close-knit group with whom they can share personal needs and joys. Activities in this curriculum will help class members get to know one another better and care for one another more as they study the Bible and apply its truths to their lives. As people reveal their thoughts and feelings to one another, they'll grow closer and develop more commitment to the group. And they'll be encouraging one another along the way!

● **An Element of Delight.** We don't often think about Jesus' ministry in this way, but he often brought fun and delight to his followers. Remember the time he raised Peter's mother-in-law or the time he sat happily with children on his lap? How about the joy and excitement at his triumphal entry into Jerusalem or the time he helped his disciples catch a boatload of fish—after they'd fished all night with no success?

People learn more when they're having fun. So within Apply-It-To-Life Adult Bible Curriculum, elements of fun and delight pop up often. And sometimes adding fun is as simple as using a carrot for a pretend microphone!

Taking the Fear out of Teaching

Teachers love Apply-It-To-Life Adult Bible Curriculum because it makes teaching much less stressful. Lessons in this curriculum...

● **are easy to teach.** Interactive learning frees the teacher from being a dispenser of information to serve as a facilitator of learning. Teachers can spend class time guiding people to discover and apply biblical truths. The studies provide clear, understandable Bible background; easy-to-prepare learning experiences; and thought-provoking discussion questions.

● **can be prepared quickly.** Lessons in Apply-It-To-Life Adult Bible Curriculum are logical and clear. There's no sorting through tons of information to figure out the lesson. In 30 minutes, a busy teacher can easily read a lesson and prepare to teach it. In addition, optional and For Extra Time activities allow the teacher to tailor the lesson to the class. And the thorough instructions and questions will guide even an inexperienced teacher through each powerful lesson.

● **let everyone share in the class' success.** With Apply-It-To-Life Adult Bible Curriculum, the teacher is one of the participants. The teacher still guides the class, but the burden is not as heavy. Everyone participates and adds to the study's effectiveness. So when the study has an impact, everyone shares in that success.

● **lead the teacher to new discoveries.** Each lesson is designed to help the teacher first discover a biblical truth. And most teachers will make additional discoveries as they prepare each lesson. In class, the teacher will discover even more as other adults share what they have found. As with any type of teaching, the teacher will likely learn more than anyone else in the class!

● **provide relevant information to class members.** Photocopiable handouts are designed to help people better understand or interpret Bible passages. And the handouts make teaching easier because the teacher can often refer to them for small-group discussion questions and instructions.

First familiarize yourself with an Apply-It-To-Life Adult Bible Curriculum lesson. The following explanations will help you understand how the lesson elements work together.

Lesson Elements

● The **Opening** maps out the lesson's agenda and introduces the topic for the session. Sometimes this activity will help people get better acquainted as they begin to explore the topic together.

● The **Bible Exploration and Application** activities will help people discover what the Bible says about the topic and how the lesson's point applies to their lives. In these varied activities, class members find answers to the "So what?" question. They discover the relevance of the Scriptures and commit to growing closer to God.

You may use one or both of the options in this section. They are designed to stand alone or to work together. Both present the same point in different ways. "For Even Deeper Discussion" questions appear at the end of each activity in this section. Use these questions whenever you feel they might be particularly helpful for your class.

● The **Closing** pulls everything in the lesson together and often funnels the lesson's message into a time of reflection and prayer.

● The **For Extra Time** section is just that. Use it when you've completed the lesson and still have time left or when you've used one Bible Exploration and Application option and don't have time to do the other. Or you might plan to use it instead of another option.

When you put all the sections together, you get a lesson that's fun and easy to teach. Plus, participants will learn truths they'll remember and apply to their daily lives.

Guidelines for a Successful Adult Class

● **Be a facilitator, not a lecturer.** Your job is to direct the activities and facilitate the discussions. You become a choreographer of sorts: someone who gets everyone else involved in the discussion and keeps the discussion on track.

● **Teach adults how to form small groups.** Help adults form groups of four, three, or two—whatever the activity calls for. Small-group sharing allows for more discussion and involvement by all participants. It's not as threatening or scary to open up to two people as it would be to 20 or 200!

Some leaders decide not to form small groups because they want to hear everybody's ideas. The intention is good, but some people just won't talk in a large group. Use a "report back" time after small-group discussions to gather the best responses from all groups.

Try creative group-forming methods to help everyone in the class get to know one another. For example, have class members form groups with others who are wearing the same color, shop at the same grocery store, were born the same month, or like the same season of the year.

● **Encourage relationship building.** George Barna, in his insightful book about the church, *The Frog in the Kettle,* explains that adults today have a strong need to develop friendships. In a society of high-tech toys, "personal" computers, and lonely commutes, people long for positive human contact. That's where our church classes and groups can jump in. Help adults form friendships through your class. What's discovered in a classroom setting will be better applied when friends support each other outside the classroom. In fact, the relationships begun in your class may be as important as the truths you help your adults learn.

● **Expect the unexpected.** Active learning is an adventure that doesn't always take you where you think you're going. Be open to the different directions the Holy Spirit may lead your class. When something goes wrong or an unexpected emotion is aroused, take advantage of this teachable moment. Ask probing questions; follow up on someone's deep need.

What should you do if people go off on a tangent? Don't panic. People learn best when they're engaged in meaningful discussion. And if you get through even one activity, your class will discover the point for the whole lesson. So relax. It's OK if you don't get everything done.

● **Participate—and encourage participation.** Apply-It-To-Life Adult Bible Curriculum is only as interactive as you and your class make it. Jump into discussions yourself, but don't "take over." Encourage everyone to participate. Use "active listening" responses such as rephrasing and summing up what's been said. To get more out of your discussions, use follow-up inquiries such as "Can you tell me more?" "What do you mean by that?" or "What makes you feel that way?" The more people participate, the more they'll discover God's truths for themselves.

● **Trust the Holy Spirit.** All the previous guidelines and the instructions in the lessons will be irrelevant if you ignore the presence of God in your classroom. God sent the Holy Spirit as our helper. As you use this curriculum, ask the Holy Spirit to help you facilitate the lessons. And ask the Holy Spirit to direct your class toward God's truth. Trust that God's Spirit can work through each person's discoveries, not just the teacher's.

How to Use This Course

Before the Four-Week Session
● Read the Course Introduction and This Course at a Glance (pp. 11-12).
● Decide how you'll use the art on the Publicity Page (p. 13) to publicize the course. Prepare fliers, newsletter articles, and posters as needed.
● Look at the Fellowship and Outreach Specials (pp. 63-64) and decide which ones you'll use.

Before Each Lesson
● Read the one-sentence Point, the Objectives, and the Bible Basis for

the lesson. The Bible Basis provides background information on the lesson's passages and shows how those passages relate to people today.

● Choose which activities you'll use from the lesson. Remember, it's not necessary to do every activity. Pick the ones that best fit your group and time allotment.

● Gather necessary supplies and make photocopies of any handouts you intend to use. They're listed in This Lesson at a Glance.

● Read each section of the lesson. Adjust activities as necessary to fit your class size and meeting room, but be careful not to delete all the activity. People learn best when they're actively involved.

● Make one photocopy of the "Apply-It-To-Life This Week!" handout for each class member.

COURSE INTRODUCTION—GENESIS: UNDERSTANDING GOD'S GOODNESS

People don't stop searching for answers to life's significant questions when they leave school and join the grown-up world. They still wonder who they are, where they came from, what their life's purpose is, why there's so much sin and suffering in the world, and who God is.

Unfortunately, the prevalence of evil in the world sometimes colors the way we look at things and leads us to false conclusions about ourselves, our world, and our God. At times, natural evils such as sickness and starvation or moral evils such as hate and violence blind us to the many evidences of God's goodness to us. That's why it's important to learn what the book of Genesis teaches about God and his goodness.

Genesis explains, for example, that the world as God created it was a good place, a paradise in which all creation enjoyed peace, health, and happiness. Evil was neither part of God's plan nor present in his original creation. But paradise was lost when Adam and Eve grew discontented with human existence and tried to become like God. According to Genesis, the presence of sin and suffering is our fault, not God's. We rejected the good life God had prepared for us to enjoy and, in so doing, introduced evil into God's perfectly good creation.

Fortunately, the story doesn't end there. Genesis also provides a word of encouragement. In spite of the presence and prevalence of evil in the world, God has not given up his commitment to make the world a good place. In fact, God is so determined to see his good will accomplished on earth that, when necessary, he'll eliminate the evil and start all over or miraculously use the evil designs of humans to further his own good plan. (For details, see Lessons 2 and 4.)

This four-week course will help people discover and apply to their lives these central theological truths of the book of Genesis. In so doing, it will enable them to recognize God's goodness even in the midst of difficult situations and to trust that God is good even when his goodness is difficult to see.

This Course at a Glance

Before you dive into the lessons, familiarize yourself with each lesson's point. Then read the Scripture passages.

- Study them to gain insight into the lessons.
- Use them as a basis for your personal devotions.
- Think about how they relate to people's situations today.

Lesson 1: It Was Very Good

The Point: God's creation was completely good until human sin corrupted it.

Bible Basis: Genesis 1:1–2:4a and 2:4b–3:24

Lesson 2: But Noah Found Favor

The Point: Sometimes God eliminates what is evil to preserve what is good.

Bible Basis: Genesis 6:5–9:3

Lesson 3: I Will Bless You

The Point: God keeps his promises to us even when we don't deserve it.

Bible Basis: Genesis 12:1–13:2

Lesson 4: God Planned It for Good

The Point: God can transform human evil into his good.

Bible Basis: Genesis 39:1-23 and 50:15-21

Grab your congregation's attention! Add the vital details to the ready-made flier below, photocopy it, and use it to advertise this course on Genesis. Insert the flier in your bulletins. Enlarge it to make posters. Splash the art or anything else from this page in newsletters, bulletins, or even on postcards! It's that simple.

The art from this page is also available on Group's MinistryNet™ computer on-line resource for you to manipulate on your computer. Call **800-447-1070** *for information.*

GENESIS: UNDERSTANDING GOD'S GOODNESS

A four-week adult course on the important truths of the first book of the Bible.

COME TO

ON

AT

COME EXPLORE THE MANY EVIDENCES OF GOD'S GOODNESS IN THE WORLD TODAY!

Apply·It·To·Life™
Adult
BIBLE CURRICULUM
from Group

Permission to photocopy this page granted for local church use. Copyright © Group Publishing, Inc., Box 481, Loveland, CO 80539.

It Was Very Good

God's creation was completely good until human sin corrupted it.

OBJECTIVES

Participants will
- examine the key truths of the biblical teaching on the creation,
- discuss the essential goodness of God's creation, and
- discover what the Bible teaches about sin and its effects.

BIBLE BASIS

Look up the Scriptures for this lesson. Then read the following background paragraphs to see how the passages relate to people today.

Genesis 1:1–2:4a teaches that God created the world without effort and without evil.

The Bible begins with a simple truth: "In the beginning God created the heavens and the earth" (Genesis 1:1, New International Version). Unfortunately, sometimes Christians spend so much time debating details about *how* God created the universe that we lose sight of other important issues.

For example, Genesis 1:1–2:4a asserts that God effortlessly brought everything into existence. Creation neither taxed nor tired God. He simply spoke the universe into existence (1:3, 6, 9, 11, 14, 20, 24). By way of contrast, the *Enuma Elish,* a Babylonian story of creation, taught that the god Marduk killed the goddess Tiamat and then shaped her corpse into the different parts of the universe. Nothing could be further from the biblical perspective. One of the clear and certain biblical affirmations is that God created all that exists easily and effortlessly.

Genesis 1:1–2:4a also teaches that God's original creation was entirely free from evil. The *Enuma Elish* pre-

GENESIS 1:1–2:4A

The systematic nature of God's forming and filling is shown by the correlation between the days. God created light and darkness on the first day and made the sun and moon on the fourth day. God separated water from sky on the second day and created fish and birds (water and sky animals) on the fifth day. On the third day, God divided the waters from the earth and produced vegetation; on the sixth day, he created the earth creatures that needed vegetation to eat, namely, animals and humans.

sents the universe as an evil place, the remnants of a defeated goddess, but the Bible offers a completely different perspective. On seven different occasions God looked at his handiwork and saw that it was good (1:4, 10, 12, 18, 21, 25, 31). In addition, God systematically transformed the chaos described in Genesis 1:2 ("a formless void," New Revised Standard Version) into an orderly cosmos. On the first three days, God *formed* the creation. Then, on days four through six, God *filled* what he had formed. The outcome of these "efforts" was a universe that was "very good" (1:31).

GENESIS 2:4B–3:24

Genesis 2:4b–3:24 reveals that humans brought all kinds of evil into the world when they tried to become like God.

The creation account contained in Genesis 2 offers a slightly different perspective on God's creative activity. While Genesis 1 presents God as a powerful deity who spoke the entire universe into existence, Genesis 2 portrays God as a potter who is personally and intimately involved in the shaping of his creation (verses 7, 19). God even draws close enough to breathe life into the nostrils of the first human (verse 7). In spite of these (and other) differences, Genesis 2 agrees that God's original creation was completely good. By the end of chapter 2, man and woman possess all they need to live in perfect harmony with God, each other, and the world.

However, the good life described in Genesis 2 no longer exists, so the story can't end there. To explain the presence of evil in the world, Genesis 3 teaches that the first humans introduced every kind of evil into God's good creation when they disobeyed God. Humans became alienated from God, each other, and their environment when they violated the order of God's creation.

Genesis 3 also explains why Adam and Eve disobeyed God and ate from the tree of knowledge of good and evil: They wanted to become like God. They desired "knowledge of good and evil"—that is, total moral knowledge—so they could make their own moral decisions. Adam and Eve hungered for independence from God, so they seized the moral knowledge that would make them like God (verses 5, 22). Not content with being human, the first humans sought to become God's equals by grasping God's knowledge. In so doing, they forfeited the idyllic human life that God had originally created for them to enjoy.

In all probability, Christians will never fully agree about all the details of the creation. However, we should be able to agree that all of creation was entirely good until human sin corrupted it. Use this lesson to help your class members appreciate the essential goodness of God's creation and to understand how human sin has infected that good creation with evil.

THIS LESSON AT A GLANCE

Section	Minutes	What Participants Will Do	Supplies
OPENING	up to 10	PERSONAL ORIGINS—Discuss how they've been affected by past experiences.	
BIBLE EXPLORATION AND APPLICATION	30 to 35	☐ Option 1: ESSENTIAL TRUTHS—Discuss what they believe about creation and examine Genesis 1:1–2:4a to discover the basic biblical teachings on the creation.	Bibles, "From Chaos to Cosmos" handouts (p. 24), "A Definite Pattern" handouts (p. 25), paper, pencils
	30 to 40	☐ Option 2: PERFECT WORLDS—Draw "perfect worlds," study Genesis 2:4b–3:24, and discuss the effects of sin on God's perfect creation.	Bibles, newsprint, markers
CLOSING	up to 10	GOD'S GOODNESS TODAY—Thank God for the good things in their lives and ask him to transform the evil in their lives into something good.	Newsprint, marker
FOR EXTRA TIME	up to 15	ONE EVENT, TWO STORIES—Discuss the similarities and differences between Genesis 1:1–2:4a and 2:4b-25.	Bible, paper, pencils, newsprint, marker

Personal Origins

(up to 10 minutes)

Say: **Welcome to the first week of our study of the first book of the Bible: Genesis. During the next four weeks, we'll explore the significance of biblical events such as the creation and the Flood. We'll also discover what biblical figures such as Abraham and Joseph can teach us about God and his goodness.**

We'll begin today by examining what Genesis 1–3 teaches about the creation of the world and of the human race. However, before we discuss the origins of humanity in general, let's learn a little about each other's personal origins.

Have people form groups of four. Tell group members to name for each other all the places they lived before their 18th birthdays.

After five minutes, get everyone's attention. Find out who's lived in the most places, the fewest places, the most unusual place, and the place farthest from your current location. Then have group members discuss the following questions. Ask for volunteers to report their groups' responses after each question. Ask:

- **What was best about living in the places you lived? worst?**

- **How have your personal origins shaped who you are today?**

- **How has your life been influenced by the experiences of your parents? your grandparents? your ancestors before them?**

Say: **Though sometimes we tend to forget it, we're all affected by what has happened in the past. To some degree, we're not only influenced by the past experiences and circumstances of our own lives but by those of the people who preceded us as well. So today we're going to examine Genesis 1–3 to discover how we've been affected by events associated with the creation of the universe. In so doing, we'll learn**

THE POINT ▶ **that ▶ the creation was completely good until human sin corrupted it.**

□ OPTION 1:
Essential Truths
(30 to 35 minutes)

Before class, make one photocopy of the "From Chaos to Cosmos" handout (p. 24) for every two class members and one photocopy of the "Definite Pattern" handout (p. 25) for every two class members.

Have people remain in their foursomes. Give each group a sheet of paper and a pencil. Tell group members they have five minutes to compose a group statement about creation. Suggest that group members brainstorm all the things they believe about creation and then vote on each idea. Groups should include in their statements only those ideas that a majority of group members believe.

After five minutes, ask groups to report their statements to the rest of the class. Then instruct group members to discuss the following questions. Ask:

- **In what ways are the statements alike? different?**

- **How can we account for the similarities? the differences?**

- **What does this reveal about Christians' views on creation?**

- **Why do you think there is a diversity of opinions on creation?**

Say: **At times, it seems that the only discussion about creation is that between people who believe in creation and those who believe in evolution. However, people who believe in creation don't always agree with one another. Because there are a number of different views among people who believe in creation, it's helpful to go back to the biblical text to discover the essential truths of the biblical teaching on creation.**

Instruct group members to number off by fours. Then have the ones, twos, threes, and fours go to different areas of the room. Give a copy of the "From Chaos to Cosmos" handout to everyone in the ones and twos and a copy of the "Definite Pattern" handout to everyone in the threes and fours. Tell groups they have 10 minutes to complete the instructions at the top of the handout.

After 10 minutes, instruct people to return to their original groups and report what they've discovered. Allow five minutes of reporting, then instruct group members to discuss the following questions. Ask:

TEACHER TIP

Groups will probably want more than five minutes to complete their statements. Although you may allow them additional time to do so, the goal of this part of the activity is to help people experience the diversity of opinions Christians hold regarding creation not to reach a group consensus.

BIBLE INSIGHT

Many scholars regard Genesis 1:1 as a summary heading to 1:2–2:4a. If this view is correct, verse 2 describes the condition of "the earth" when God began to create it. That is, verse 2 teaches that the visible universe was formless and empty before God formed it (days 1-3) and filled it (days 4-6).

Biblical scholars have also observed the following literary pattern in Genesis 1:1–2:4a:

- **Announcement:** "God said" (1:3, 6, 9, 11, 14, 20, 24, 26)
- **Command:** "Let there be" (1:3, 6, 9, 11, 14, 15, 20, 24)
- **Result:** "and there was" or "and it was so" (1:3, 7, 9, 11, 15, 24, 30)
- **Evaluation:** "God saw that it was good" (1:4, 10, 12, 18, 21, 25, 31)
- **Time marker:** "There was evening and morning" (1:5, 8, 13, 19, 23, 31)

This pattern emphasizes the systematic and orderly manner in which God created all that exists.

Since this option focuses almost entirely on creation, you may want to supplement it with a discussion of the entrance of sin and evil into God's creation. If you don't complete Option 2, have groups read Genesis 3:1-19 and answer the last five questions of Option 2.

THE POINT ▷

- How fully do we agree on the biblical teaching on creation?

- What are the clear biblical teachings about creation? What questions remain unanswered?

- What can we do to increase our level of agreement?

- How should we deal with issues about which we continue to disagree?

Say: **At the very least, we should be able to agree that the original creation was completely good. Moreover, if we accept the clear teaching of Genesis 3, we should agree that ▷ human sin corrupted God's good creation. If we focus on these two foundational truths, we'll be less prone to argue about our differences of opinion and better prepared to grow in our knowledge and appreciation of God and his creation.**

■■■■■■■■■■■■■■■■■■■■■■■■■■■■■

FOR *Even Deeper* DISCUSSION

Form groups of four or fewer to discuss the following questions:

- Read Genesis 1:26-27. What does it mean that we are made in God's image? What is the relationship between the image of God and our responsibility to rule the rest of creation?

- Read Genesis 1:26-28 and 2:15. What rights do we have as "rulers" of creation? What responsibilities? How does God want us to balance our rights and our responsibilities?

■■■■■■■■■■■■■■■■■■■■■■■■■■■■■

☐ **OPTION 2:**
Perfect Worlds

(30 to 40 minutes)

Form groups of four. Give each group a sheet of newsprint and several markers. Say: **You have five minutes to draw a picture that represents your group's idea of a "perfect world." Begin by discussing in your group what a perfect world would look like. Then have one or more of your group members draw that perfect world on the sheet of newsprint.**

After five minutes, ask groups to display and to explain their drawings to the rest of the class. Then have group members discuss the following questions. Ask:

- How easy was it to imagine a perfect world? to draw it?

- **What similarities do our perfect worlds share? In what ways are they different?**

- **What do our perfect worlds reveal about us as creators?**

- **How do our perfect worlds compare with the real world?**

Ask for volunteers to summarize their groups' responses to the questions. Then have each group read **Genesis 2:4b-25** and list on the newsprint any noteworthy characteristics of the Garden of Eden.

After five minutes, ask groups to report what they've learned. Then have group members discuss the following questions. Ask for volunteers to report their groups' answers after each question. Ask:

- **What words would you use to describe the original creation?**

- **What does the original creation reveal about God as Creator?**

- **How are our perfect worlds like God's original creation? How are they different?**

- **How is the world today like God's original creation? How is it different?**

Read **Genesis 1:31** aloud. Then say: **The first two chapters of Genesis characterize the world as very good, but it's unlikely God would say the same thing about the world today. This should lead us to ask: If God created the world completely good, why do we see evil around us today?**

Instruct groups to read **Genesis 3:1-19.** After every group has read the passage, tell groups to wad up their sheets of newsprint tightly. Then have each group unfold its newsprint and discuss the following questions. Ask:

- **How is what happened to our pictures like what happened to God's perfect world? How is it different?**

- **What words would you use to describe the creation after sin entered it?**

- **What evidences of goodness do you still see in God's creation? in your life?**

- **In what specific ways can you show appreciation to God for these good things?**

- **What signs of moral or natural evil do you see in the world today? in your life?**

- **In what specific ways can you overcome that evil with good?**

T E A C H E R
TIP

You may want to hang a sheet of newsprint where everyone can see it and record characteristics of the Garden of Eden on it as class members list them.

T E A C H E R
TIP

Suggest that groups cross off any characteristics written on their newsprint that are no longer true of the world today. That will help people *see* how greatly the world has changed from its original condition.

BIBLE
I N S I G H T

It's important to understand the difference between moral evil and natural evil. Any deviation from God's character or will is evil, but there are different kinds of evil. Evil includes everything sinful (moral evil) and everything harmful to God's creation (natural evil). Suffering, conflict, death, and destruction are examples of natural evil. Although sin brought natural evil into God's good creation, one cannot always link a specific instance of natural evil—for example, the death of a child—with a particular sin. Often we suffer simply because we live in a world infected by sin and death.

Ask for volunteers to report their groups' ideas for overcoming evil with good, then say: **Though we may disagree about some details concerning the "how" of creation, we should be able to agree that ▷ the creation was completely good until human sin corrupted it. And, with that basic truth as our common foundation, we should encourage each other to appreciate what's still good about God's creation and to overcome any evil that we encounter with the goodness of God.**

■ ■

For *Even Deeper* Discussion

Form groups of four or fewer to discuss the following questions:

● Read Genesis 2:17 and 3:4-6, 22. What is "the knowledge of good and evil"? Why did Eve and Adam want this knowledge? What does this imply about the nature or essence of sin? How have you attempted to usurp God's place in your life?

● Read Genesis 3:14-19. To what extent should we attempt to alleviate results of sin such as pain in childbirth? the subordination of women? toilsome labor?

● Read Genesis 3:21-24. To what extent are God's actions in these verses punishment? to what extent protection? What do these actions reveal about God?

■ ■

Apply·It·To·Life™ *This Week!*

The "Apply-It-To-Life This Week!" handout (p. 26) helps people further explore the issues uncovered in today's class. Give everyone a photocopy of the handout. Encourage class members to take time during the coming week to explore the questions and activities on the handout.

CLOSING

God's Goodness Today
(up to 10 minutes)

Have people remain in their groups from the previous activity. Say: **Genesis 1–3 teaches that ▷ human sin corrupted God's good creation, but that doesn't mean that evil has triumphed. God still gives us good things,**

and he often transforms the evil that surrounds us into something good.

Ask the entire class to name evidences of God's goodness in their lives. For example, someone might name a friend, report a pay raise at work, mention an answer to prayer, or describe a pleasant time spent with family. List the responses on a sheet of newsprint. Encourage everyone to identify at least three evidences of God's goodness.

After five minutes, have each group member name an area in his or her life that's been damaged by sin. Group members don't need to identify the sin or whether it was their sin or someone else's. After everyone in the group has named an area, have group members close the lesson in prayer, thanking God for the good things he's brought into their lives and asking him to transform the evil in their lives into something good.

For Extra Time

ONE EVENT, TWO STORIES

(up to 15 minutes)

Form groups of four. Give each group a sheet of paper and a pencil. Assign half the groups Genesis 1:1–2:4a and half Genesis 2:4b-25. Have groups answer these questions as they read their passages:

- In what order are things created?
- By what means does God create things?
- How long does the process of creation take?
- What is the condition of the finished product?

After 10 minutes, have groups report their answers. Record their responses on a sheet of newsprint. Then ask the entire class the following questions:

- **How are the two accounts of creation similar? different?**

- **How can we best explain the similarities? the differences?**

- **How does the presence of two accounts help us identify the essentials of the biblical teaching on creation?**

From Chaos to Cosmos

Within your group, read Genesis 1:1–2:4a and the FYI box below. Then follow the instructions and answer the questions to complete your handout.

Read Genesis 1:1–2:4a again, and list in the appropriate places the details of how God formed and filled the world.

FORMING	FILLING
DAY 1	DAY 4
DAY 2	DAY 5
DAY 3	DAY 6

DISCUSSION QUESTIONS:
- What's the connection between what was formed on day 1 and what was filled on day 4? between days 2 and 5? between days 3 and 6?
- What does the forming-and-filling pattern imply about God? about the creation?
- Based on your study, what are your conclusions about the biblical teaching on creation?
- Which of your conclusions do you regard as most important? least important?

A Definite Pattern
Pattern
Pattern
Pattern
Pattern

Within your group, read Genesis 1:1–2:4a and the FYI box below. Then follow the instructions and answer the questions to complete your handout.

 Biblical scholars have observed a pattern in Genesis 1:1–2:4a that is repeated for nearly every day of creation. The five elements of the pattern are:
- Announcement: "God said"
- Command: "Let there be"
- Result: "and there was" or "and it was so"
- Evaluation: "God saw that it was good"
- Time marker: "There was evening and morning"

Patterr
Pattern
Pattern

Read Genesis 1:1–2:4a again and list...

- all the words or phrases that describe how God created things.

- all the words or phrases that describe God's evaluation of his creation.

Pattern
Pat
Pattern

Discussion QUESTIONS:
- What do the methods God used to create suggest about him?
- What does God's evaluation of his creation indicate about the creation? about him?
- Based on your study, what are you conclusions about the biblical teaching on creation?
- Which of your conclusions do you regard as most important? least important?

Apply·It·To·Life™ This Week!

It Was Very Good

God's creation was completely good
until human sin corrupted it.
Genesis 1:1–2:4a and 2:4b–3:24

Reflecting on God's Word

Each day this week, read one of the following Scriptures and examine what it teaches about the creation. Then consider how you can incorporate this teaching into your beliefs about God's creation. List your discoveries in the space under each passage.

Day 1: Job 38:1-11. God challenges Job to answer questions about creation.

Day 2: John 1:1-13. Jesus Christ is both creator and Savior of the world.

Day 3: Psalm 8:1-9. Humans are less than gods and more than animals.

Day 4: Colossians 1:15-20. Christ created all things and sustains all things.

Day 5: Jonah 4:10-11. God is concerned about every part of his creation.

Day 6: Revelation 21:1–22:5. God will restore creation to its original perfection.

Beyond Reflection

Read Genesis 1:26-30 and list all the ways you "rule" the earth, either directly or indirectly. Your rule may range from taking care of a pet to raising livestock, from tending a yard to farming for a living, or from recycling aluminum to mining coal. Then evaluate how well your rule honors God and the goodness of his creation. Use the following questions to examine each aspect of your rule:
- Is my rule constructive or destructive?
- Does my rule promote goodness or evil?
- Am I serving God's interests or my own?

Ask God to show you how you could do better and take action on any ideas for improvement. In one month, evaluate your progress and identify areas in which you need further growth.

Coming Next Week: But Noah Found Favor (Genesis 6:5–9:3)

But Noah Found Favor

Sometimes God eliminates what is evil to preserve what is good.

OBJECTIVES

Participants will
- explore how God might have felt as his creation was damaged by sin,
- discover similarities between God's original creation and the new creation after the Flood, and
- determine how they might please God and eliminate evil in their lives.

BIBLE BASIS

Look up the Scriptures for this lesson. Then read the following background paragraphs to see how the passage relates to people today.

Genesis 6:5–9:3 explains why God destroyed corrupt humanity but preserved Noah and his family.

In all probability, the ancient Israelites didn't first learn of a worldwide flood when they read about it in the book of Genesis. In fact, several of the cultures that preceded or surrounded ancient Israel had their own versions of such a cataclysmic event, and it's likely that the Israelites were aware of these other accounts. In the Sumerian account, Ziusudra was the sole survivor of the flood. One Babylonian version claims that Atrahasis, his family, some artisans, and many animals survived the flood in an ark. However, the Babylonian story known as *The Gilgamesh Epic* states that Utnapishtim built an ark to preserve human and animal life from certain death in a universal

GENESIS 6:5–9:3

BIBLE INSIGHT

Alexander Heidel presents translations and summaries of these and other ancient Near Eastern flood accounts in *The Gilgamesh Epic and Old Testament Parallels* (Chicago: University of Chicago Press, 1949). Heidel also discusses the theological differences between the biblical and extrabiblical accounts.

flood. Although these accounts resemble the biblical version of the Flood in significant ways, they promote views of God and humanity that are incompatible with a biblical worldview. Therefore, Genesis 6–9 was probably written to teach the truth about the Flood and not merely to introduce the Israelites to it.

According to Genesis 6:5-13, for example, God sent the Flood because humans were evil, not because they were so noisy that he couldn't sleep (as Atrahasis reports). Wickedness so permeated the human race that people were constantly and completely inclined to evil (6:5). And as though corrupting themselves were not bad enough, people also contaminated the creation. God wanted humans to "fill" the earth with people (1:28), but Noah's generation "filled" it with violence instead (6:11).

Contrary to what one might expect (and unlike the gods of the extrabiblical accounts), God responded to this moral devolution with anguish instead of anger. As human hearts filled with evil, God's heart filled with pain, and eventually the increase and spread of human sin brought God such grief that he regretted having created humans (6:6-7). Even then, God's decision to punish humanity was neither easy nor pleasant. God preferred to let everyone live (see Ezekiel 18:23), but Noah was the only person righteous enough to warrant it. So God determined to destroy everyone but Noah and his family in a flood.

The Flood served several purposes. As in the other ancient Near Eastern accounts, the Flood in Genesis effectively killed every living thing. But it's also possible that the flood was intended to purify the blood-stained earth. Since the blood of a murder victim polluted the ground (Numbers 35:30-33; see Genesis 4:10-11), it's reasonable to think that God sent the flood waters to cleanse the earth from the blood shed during those violent times (6:11-13). That would explain why God chose to drown every living thing and didn't merely destroy sinful humanity.

Furthermore, the Flood returned the earth to its precreation condition as a watery chaos. The clear parallels between Genesis 1 and the description of the Flood imply that God flooded the earth so he could then re-create it. As in Genesis 1:2, the water-covered earth was formless and lifeless (7:18-22). Moreover, the creative process began when God's "wind"—in Hebrew, the same word as "Spirit" in 1:2—went over the waters covering the earth (8:1). Finally, God repeated to Noah and his family many of the commands he had given the first human couple long before (9:1-3, compare 1:28-30). Therefore, we may conclude that God flooded the earth to destroy sinful humanity, to purify the bloodstained ground, and to prepare for his re-creation of the world according to his good plan.

No one enjoys discipline or the loss that often accompanies it, but eventually everyone feels its sting. When that happens, it's easy to become angry with God and bitter about the pain he's brought into our lives. However, God isn't like the authority figures from our past who may have disciplined us out of anger or revenge. God disciplines us for our good, so he can eliminate what is evil and preserve what is good. Use this lesson to help your class members understand how and why God sometimes takes strong measures to combat the sin in their lives and in the world around them.

THIS LESSON AT A GLANCE

Section	Minutes	What Participants Will Do	Supplies
OPENING	up to 10	**A GREAT GARDEN**—Share gardening experiences and discuss how weeds and insects can inhibit growth.	
BIBLE EXPLORATION AND APPLICATION	25 to 35	☐ Option 1: **DAMAGED GOODS**—Create something out of clay, have others damage it, and compare the damage to humans' damaging of God's creation through sin as described in Genesis 6:5-13.	Bibles, modeling clay or dough, newsprint, marker, tape
	20 to 30	☐ Option 2: **A NEW CREATION**—Examine similarities between God's original creation in Genesis 1 and his new creation after the flood as described in Genesis 6:5–9:3.	Bibles, "God's New Creation" handouts (p. 36), newsprint, marker
CLOSING	up to 10	**FAITHFULLY OBEDIENT**—Examine how Noah found favor with God and determine to work on areas in their lives where they can please God more.	Bibles
FOR EXTRA TIME	up to 15	**OTHER VIEWS**—Explore passages throughout the Bible that talk about Noah.	Bibles
	up to 10	**WHAT IF?**—Discuss how our outlook and faith might change if Noah's ark were discovered.	

A Great Garden

(up to 10 minutes)

Begin class by having people raise their hands if they have any gardening experience. Then form groups of three to six, with at least one gardener in each group. Have group members discuss the following questions. Ask:

- **What's been your most enjoyable experience with a garden?**
- **What's been your most frustrating experience with a garden?**
- **What's the hardest part of growing a productive garden?**
- **What happens if you let weeds grow wild in your garden?**
- **What happens if you let destructive insects or worms inhabit your garden?**

Then say: **In some ways, the world is like a garden, with God as its gardener. God wants the world to be a healthy and productive place, but he knows that certain things will destroy his creation and make growth difficult for people who want to serve him.** **▷So sometimes God eliminates what is evil to preserve what is good. This week, in our second study from the book of Genesis, we're going to examine what God did in sending a flood to destroy the evil on earth.**

T H E   P O I N T ▷

TEACHER
TIP

Making your own modeling dough is easy. In a large bowl, mix together 1 cup of cold water, 1 cup of salt, and 2 teaspoons of cooking oil. Then gradually work 3 cups of flour and 2 tablespoons of corn starch into the mixture. If you want, add several drops of food coloring. Knead until thoroughly mixed. If the dough is too sticky, add a little flour. If it's too dry, add a little water.

BIBLE EXPLORATION AND APPLICATION

☐ **O P T I O N   1 :**
Damaged Goods

(25 to 35 minutes)

Form groups of six to eight. Give everyone a piece of modeling clay or modeling dough about the size of a baseball. Tell people they have three minutes to make a model of something they really like or enjoy. After three minutes, have people show their creations and tell what they represent.

Then say: **Now we're going to pass our creations around our groups. As each one comes to you, do something destructive to it.**

After the creations go around the groups and return to their owners, have groups read **Genesis 6:5-13.** Then have people discuss the following questions in their groups. After each question, ask for volunteers to report their groups' responses. Ask:

- **What was it like to see people destroying your creation?**

- **How are your feelings like what God felt as people damaged his creation? How are they different?**

- **How is the condition of your creation similar to the condition of God's creation just prior to the Flood? How is it different?**

Instruct group members to number off by threes. Have the ones, twos, and threes gather in separate areas of the room. Assign each of these new groups one of the following passages: **Genesis 7:6-12; 7:20–8:5; 8:13-19.** Tell groups to read their passages and discuss the following questions. To help groups remember the questions, write them on a sheet of newsprint and hang it in a prominent location.

- What are the key events or ideas in this passage?
- How do these events relate to God's elimination of evil?
- How do these events relate to God's preservation of good?

After about five minutes, have people return to their original groups and report on their discussions of the passages. After people report, say: **Now look at what remains of your clay creation. Examine it carefully, then recreate it into what you made the first time. You have three minutes to remake your creation.**

After people remake their creations, instruct group members to discuss the following questions. Ask:

- **How did the remake of your clay creation turn out?**

- **How is this similar to God's remaking of the world with Noah and Noah's family? How is it different?**

Say:  **Sometimes God eliminates what's evil to preserve what's good. That's what happened in Noah's day, but it happens today as well.**

Have the entire class discuss the following questions. Ask:

- **How is the world today similar to the world just prior to the Flood?**

- **How do you think God feels about the condition of the world today?**

- **How might God want to eliminate the evil in today's world?**

- **How do you think God wants us to respond to the evil we see around us?**

◄ THE POINT

TEACHER TIP

It's important to say The Point as it's written or in your own words in each activity. Stating it repeatedly helps people remember it and apply it to their lives.

As people respond to the prior question, list their suggestions on a chalkboard or newsprint. Encourage people to be specific. Save the list for use in the Closing.

Say: **As long as there are people in this world, there will be evil. But God wants ▷ to eliminate evil so he can preserve what is good. As we oppose evil and promote good in the world today, we'll be working with God to accomplish his will on earth.**

THE POINT▷

■■■■■■■■■■■■■■■■■■■■■■■■■■■■■■

FOR *Even Deeper*
DISCUSSION

Form groups of four or fewer to discuss the following questions:

● What do you think displeases God most about today's world? What displeases him most about Christians? What pleases him most about Christians?

● How might God eliminate evil in our world? How would that elimination of evil help preserve what is good?

● Read Genesis 8:20-22. What does this passage say about the future of the world?

■■■■■■■■■■■■■■■■■■■■■■■■■■■■■■

□ **OPTION 2:**
A New Creation
(20 to 30 minutes)

Before class, make one photocopy of the "God's New Creation" handout (p. 36) for every three class members.

BIBLE
INSIGHT

The Hebrew word that most English versions translate "Spirit" in Genesis 1:2 is the same as that translated "wind" in Genesis 8:1. This word can be translated either "spirit" or "wind," as many Old Testament passages demonstrate. To make the parallel between Genesis 1:2 and 8:1 more evident, one should probably use the same English word—"Spirit" or "wind"—in both verses. See, for example, the New Revised Standard Version.

Form three groups. If you have 18 or more people, form six or more groups of three to six people each. If you didn't do Option 1, have people begin by reading **Genesis 6:15-13; 7:6-12; 7:20–8:5;** and **8:13-19** within their groups.

Say: **After God destroyed the earth with a flood, he started over with a new creation. Let's look at the similarities between God's original creation and the Bible's description of the Flood.**

Give each group a copy of the "God's New Creation" handout. Assign each group one section from the handout. Tell groups they have five minutes to complete the instructions for their sections.

After five minutes, ask groups to report their findings. Then ask the entire class:

● **Why did God destroy the creation he'd made and start over with a new one?**

● **Why did God preserve Noah and his family?**

- How were things the same for Noah's family after the Flood? How were they different?

- How would things be different for us if God removed all the evil around us?

Have people discuss the following questions in their groups. After each question, ask for volunteers to report their groups' responses. Ask:

- In what ways does God eliminate evil from our lives?

- How has God eliminated evil from your life in the past? How did this help preserve what is good?

- What things in your life might God want to eliminate today?

- How can we seek to get rid of the evil within our own lives? avoid the evil around us?

After about five minutes, have groups report their responses. As they report their answers to the last two questions, list their responses on a sheet of newsprint. If you did Option 1, add the responses to the list you already made. If possible, list a total of at least six to eight responses.

Then say: ▶ **God sometimes eliminates evil, as he did in Noah's day, to preserve what is good. Therefore, we should allow God to work in our lives, eliminating anything evil so we can grow in our relationship with him.**

◀ **T H E   P O I N T**

■ ■

For *Even Deeper* DISCUSSION

Form groups of four or fewer to discuss the following questions:

- What does the prevalence of evil in Noah's day tell us about people? What does it tell us about God?

- What does God's sending of the Flood demonstrate about his goodness? What else does it tell us about God? Why do you think God sometimes eliminates evil and sometimes allows it to go on?

■ ■

Apply·It·To·Life™ *This Week!*

The "Apply-It-To-Life This Week!" handout (p. 37) helps people further explore the issues uncovered in today's class. Give everyone a photocopy of the handout. Encourage class members to take time during the coming week to explore the questions and activities on the handout.

Faithfully Obedient

(up to 10 minutes)

THE POINT ▷

Say: **One verse we haven't considered to this point provides insight into why Noah found favor with God. Let's take a look at Genesis 6:22.**

Have someone read **Genesis 6:22** aloud. Then say: **Even when God told him to do something unheard of—build an ark—Noah responded in complete faith and obedience. Noah was declared righteous and was kept from death because he had faith, even though he was surrounded by evil.** ▷**Sometimes God wipes out what is evil to preserve what is good. God did so in Noah's day, and he will do so in our lives as we follow Noah's example of seeking to please God.**

Form pairs and direct people's attention to the list you made during Option 1 or Option 2. Say: **This list gives ways we can please God and eliminate detrimental things in our lives. Look over the list and choose one area where you could improve. Tell your partner what you want to work on and pray about it together, asking God to help you get rid of anything in your life that could damage your relationship with him.**

When everyone has prayed, end class by encouraging people to follow through on the commitments they've made.

For Extra Time

OTHER VIEWS

(up to 15 minutes)

To get a better idea of Noah's character, explore other Scripture passages that mention him. Form groups of four and have groups examine as many of the following passages as you have time for: Genesis 9:20-27; Ezekiel 14:12-20; Matthew 24:36-39; Hebrews 11:7; 1 Peter 3:18-22; 2 Peter 2:4-9. Have people answer these questions for each passage:

● What does this passage tell us about Noah?
● What does this passage tell us about God?
● What does this passage tell us about the relationship between God and Noah?

WHAT IF?

(up to 10 minutes)

Read the following statement and discuss the questions below it. Say: **Some people are convinced that**

Noah's ark still exists and has been sighted high in the mountains of Ararat in Turkey. Ask:

- What if this claim were proven to be true? How would it affect the way you look at the Bible? your confidence in your beliefs?

- What if this claim were proven to be false? How might it affect the way you look at the Bible? your confidence in your beliefs?

GOD'S NEW CREATION

SECTION 1

Compare Genesis 1:2 with Genesis 7:18-22. Then answer the questions below.

● How was the earth similar in these two passages? How was it different?

● What was God preparing to do by covering the earth with water?

SECTION 2

Read the information in the FYI box and compare Genesis 1:2 with Genesis 8:1-2. Then answer the questions below.

● In what ways are these passages similar? How are they different?

● What do the similarities imply about what God was doing after he flooded the earth?

> **F.Y.I.**
>
> The Hebrew word that most English versions translate "Spirit" in Genesis 1:2 is the same as that translated "wind" in Genesis 8:1. This word can be translated either "spirit" or "wind," as many Old Testament passages demonstrate. To make the parallel between Genesis 1:2 and 8:1 more evident, one should probably use the same English word—"Spirit" or "wind"—in both verses.

SECTION 3

Compare Genesis 1:28-30 with Genesis 9:1-3.

● In what ways are these passages similar? How are they different?

● How was the world after the Flood like the original creation? How was it different?

But Noah Found Favor

Sometimes God eliminates what is evil
to preserve what is good.
Genesis 6:5–9:3

Reflecting on God's Word

Each day this week, read one of the following Scriptures and examine what that passage says about the relationship between good and evil in our lives. Think about how you might apply the passages to your life. List your discoveries in the space under each passage.

Day 1: Psalm 84:10-12. God gives good things to those who trust in him.

Day 2: Hosea 2:1-23. God may use evil to lead us back to him.

Day 3: 2 Corinthians 12:7-10. God can use evil to accomplish good in our lives.

Day 4: 1 John 4:7-12. God's goodness is evident when we love one another.

Day 5: 2 Timothy 2:20-26. We should prepare ourselves to do good works.

Day 6: James 4:1-10. We must resist the devil and submit ourselves to God.

Beyond Reflection

Think about how God has used others in your life to direct you away from evil influences and toward good ones. Identify at least one individual who's been a big help to you and call or write that person to express your appreciation. If the person is no longer living, thank God for guiding you through that person.

Coming Next Week: I Will Bless You (Genesis 12:1–13:2)

I Will Bless You

God keeps his promises to us even when we don't deserve it.

◀ THE POINT

OBJECTIVES

Participants will
- discuss the effects of kept and unkept promises,
- discover that God always keeps his promises to us, and
- examine the Bible to see what God has actually promised.

BIBLE BASIS

Look up the Scriptures for this lesson. Then read the following background paragraphs to see how the passages relate to people today.

Genesis 12:1–13:2 narrates God's promise to bless Abram and Abram's endangerment of that promise.

Genesis 12 marks a turning point in the book of Genesis and in the history of God's plan to deliver humanity from sin. In Genesis 1–11, God dealt with humanity as a whole, but, beginning with Genesis 12, God focused on Abram and his descendants, the nation of Israel. However, God's selection of one man and one nation did not entail a rejection of everyone else. On the contrary, God chose Abram so he could be a channel of salvation and blessing to the people of every nation. The selection of Abram was God's answer to the escalating problem of sin described in Genesis 1–11.

When Adam and Eve introduced sin into God's creation (3:6-7), God acted both as their judge (3:8-19) and as their deliverer (3:20-24). Likewise, God responded to Cain's murder of his brother (4:8) with judgment (4:9-12) and deliverance (4:13-16). Again, God reacted to the corruption of the world during the days of Noah (6:11-12) with

GENESIS 12:1–13:2

Later in his life, Abram was known as Abraham. Genesis 17:5 explains that God changed Abram's name to Abraham to signify that he would make Abraham the father of many nations.

judgment (6:13) and deliverance (6:14-22). However, when people tried to storm heaven's gates by building the tower of Babel (11:4), God responded only in judgment (11:5-9). The pattern of sin → judgment → deliverance appeared to break down, but the final element was merely delayed. The call of Abram in Genesis 12:1-3 supplied the expected deliverance, for God promised to bless every nation through Abram (and his descendants).

God's call of Abram includes a command (12:1) and a promise (12:2-3). In context, the command ("Go!") serves as the condition of the promise. Consequently, God's promise becomes fully functional when Abram "goes" just as God had commanded him (12:4). Once he arrived in the land of promise (Canaan), Abram was completely ready to receive the benefits of God's commitment to him.

The promise itself is marked by the repetition of several key words. First, the personal pronoun "I" is the subject of five of the seven clauses that make up the promise. Because God is the "I" who is speaking, the fulfillment of the promise depends entirely on him. God has committed himself to a certain course of action, and no one (including Abram) will be able to thwart the execution of God's will. The words "bless" or "blessing" also appear five times in verses 2-3. God promises Abram specific benefits: numerous descendants, renown, and protection. But God's desire to show favor is not limited to any one man (or nation). God intends to bless Abram so that Abram can be a blessing to others.

Abram's initial response to God's promise was commendable. He journeyed to Canaan, traveled throughout the land from north to south, and claimed it for God by building altars at several key sites. Sometime later, however, Abram placed God's promise in danger by leaving the land of promise. Then, to make matters worse, he instructed Sarai, his wife, to lie about her marital status and then allowed her to be taken into Pharaoh's harem.

God's judgment against Abram's sin was swift and sure...and aimed at Pharaoh. Contrary to what one might expect, Abram didn't suffer noticeably for his misdeeds. Instead, God "plagued" Pharaoh and his household (12:17, compare with 12:3) and apparently blessed Abram with great wealth (12:16, 20; 13:1-2). Against every human expectation, God blessed Abram through the very actions by which Abram had endangered God's promise. God was so committed to his promise to bless Abram that he kept that promise even when Abram did nothing to deserve it.

In the face of incessant change and an uncertain future, people today long for security and stability. Unfortunately, all too often people seek the security they need in the insubstantial things of life: houses, jobs, or human relationships. God's Word teaches that God is the only source of real security. Use this lesson to help people understand and appreciate the security that can be found only in God and his commitment to us.

THIS LESSON AT A GLANCE

Section	Minutes	What Participants Will Do	Supplies
OPENING	up to 10	**PROMISES, PROMISES**—Discuss how broken promises affect their relationships.	
BIBLE EXPLORATION AND APPLICATION	35 to 40	☐ Option 1: **CERTAIN PROMISES**—React to undeserved rewards, discover why God blessed an undeserving Abram in Genesis 12:1–13:2, and examine some of God's promises.	Bibles, "What Has God Really Promised?" handouts (p.49), snacks, paper, pencils, tape, marker, newsprint
	25 to 35	☐ Option 2: **OUR FEARS, HIS PROMISES**—List their greatest fears, discuss God's faithfulness to Abram in Genesis 12:1–13:2, and identify biblical promises that refute their fears.	Bibles, pencils, paper, marker, newsprint, tape
CLOSING	up to 10	**HELP OUR UNBELIEF**—Discuss promises that are hard to believe and ask God to help them trust him to keep those promises.	
FOR EXTRA TIME	up to 15	**MORE PROMISES**—Examine more biblical promises to discover what God has and has not promised us.	"What Has God Really Promised?" handouts (p. 49), pencils
	up to 10	**HISTORY REPEATS ITSELF**—Compare Genesis 12:10–13:2 with 20:1-18 and 26:1-14, then discuss what the three accounts teach about God's commitment and our responsibility.	Bibles

Promises, Promises

(up to 10 minutes)

Instruct people to form groups of four. Have group members each describe a promise someone made to them but didn't keep. If possible, people should explain why the promise wasn't kept. For example, someone might say that her dad promised to come to her high school softball tournament but worked late instead; someone else might describe a friend's failure to show up for a lunch appointment.

Allow five minutes for people to share, then instruct group members to discuss the following questions. After each question, ask for volunteers to report their groups' responses. Ask:

- **How did you feel when this person broke the promise?**

- **How did the broken promise affect your relationship with the person? your opinion of the person?**

- **Have you ever felt as though God has broken a promise to you? Explain.**

- **How did this affect your relationship with God? your opinion of him?**

Say: **It's hard to trust people who have broken promises to us in the past. In the same way, it's difficult to fully trust God when we feel that he hasn't kept all his promises to us. However, today we'll discover that we can trust God completely because ▷God always keeps his promises to us.**

T H E   P O I N T ▷

BIBLE EXPLORATION AND APPLICATION

□ **OPTION 1:**

Certain Promises

(35 to 40 minutes)

Before class, make one photocopy of the "What Has God *Really* Promised?" handout (p. 49) for each person. Also, bring a healthy treat such as a piece of fruit or a snack bar for each class member. Before anyone arrives for class, set out four of the treats and place the rest where people won't be able to see them.

Keep people in their groups of four. Give each group a sheet of paper and a pencil. Say: **Let's have a competition to see which group can win the reward I've set out. I'll identify two sentences that I want each group** to write out word for word. The group that writes out the sentences most accurately wins. The two sentences are the main points from the first two lessons of this course. Go.

Allow groups three minutes to work, then ask them to report what they've written. Compare their points with the actual points for Lessons 1 and 2 (see p. 12) and declare a winner. Then bring out the treats you've hidden and distribute them to the members of the losing groups. After everyone on a losing group has a snack, give the reward you've set out to the members of the winning group.

While people are enjoying their snacks, have group members discuss the following questions. Ask for volunteers to report their groups' responses after each question. Ask:

- **How well did I keep my promise to reward the winning group?**

- **What's your reaction to my rewarding people who didn't earn it?**

- **Does God ever reward people who don't deserve it? Explain.**

- **How do you react when God rewards people who don't deserve it?**

Say: **Whether we like it or not, sometimes good things happen to bad people. Genesis 12:10–13:2, for example, describes something good happening to Abram just after he'd been bad.**

Instruct groups to read **Genesis 12:10–13:2.** While groups are reading, write the following questions on a sheet of newsprint and hang it where everyone can see it.

- In what specific ways was Abram bad?
- What good things happened to Abram?
- How did Abram's bad behavior bring him good fortune?

After everyone finishes reading, have group members discuss the questions. Allow five minutes for discussion, then ask groups to summarize their responses. After every group has reported, ask the following question of the entire class:

- **Why do you think God allowed Abram to benefit from his bad behavior?**

After several minutes of discussion, have people read **Genesis 12:1-4** and answer the preceding question again.

Say: **It's unlikely that this story was included in the Bible so we'd follow Abram's bad example. It's far more likely that we're to learn from Abram's experiences that ▶ God keeps all his promises.**

If one or more groups write out both points perfectly, declare the group that finished first the winner.

 **THE POINT**

God kept his promise to bless Abram even when Abram didn't seem worthy of blessing, and God will keep his promises to us even when we may not seem to deserve it. Knowing that our security rests in God's faithfulness, not in our ability to earn God's favor, should motivate us to examine closely what God has and has not committed himself to. That's precisely what we're going to do.

Give everyone a copy of the "What Has God *Really* Promised?" handout and a pencil. Assign each group two of the biblical passages on the handout. Have people read the instructions at the top of the handout and then work with their group members to complete their sections of the handout.

After 10 minutes, ask groups to report what they've learned. Encourage people to discuss specific promises as well as general principles about God's promises. Then have group members discuss the following questions. Ask:

- **In what ways are the promises of God similar? different?**

- **How can we keep from misunderstanding God's promises? from abusing them?**

- **What makes it difficult for you to trust God's promises?**

- **How can you increase your faith in God and his promises?**

THE POINT ▷

Say: **Sometimes people become disappointed or angry with God because they feel that he hasn't kept his promises to them. However, the Bible clearly teaches that ▷ God always keeps his promises, even when we don't deserve it. If we want to avoid being disappointed or angry with God, we need to discover precisely what God has and has not promised and then trust that God will do exactly what he's said he'll do.**

■ ■

FOR *Even Deeper* DISCUSSION

Form groups of four or fewer to discuss the following questions:

- How should the certainty of God's blessing have influenced the way Abram acted? How should the reliability of God's promises affect the way we live? our relationship with God?

- To what extent are God's promises valid for all people at all times? To what extent are some limited to certain groups? How can we tell if a biblical promise applies to us? What can we learn from promises that don't apply to us?

■■■■■■■■■■■■■■■■■■■■■■■■■■■■

☐ **O P T I O N   2 :**

Our Fears, His Promises

(25 to 35 minutes)

Have people remain in their groups of four. Give everyone a sheet of paper and a pencil. Instruct people to list on their papers their greatest fears. People may write as many fears as they want, but everyone should write at least one fear that can be shared with others.

After several minutes, have people each describe one of their fears to the rest of the group. Then have group members discuss the following questions. After each question, ask for volunteers to report their groups' responses. Ask:

● **In what ways are our fears similar? different?**

● **What do you think causes us to fear these things?**

● **How does fear affect our attitude about life? our relationship with God?**

Say: **In many cases, our fears arise from a basic insecurity in our relationship with God. We fear that somehow we can lose God's love or involvement in our lives. However, there's no reason for us to feel insecure with God. God is just as committed to us as he was to someone like Abram. Genesis 12:1–13:2 shows us how committed God was to Abram.**

Give each group a sheet of paper. Tell groups to read **Genesis 12:1–13:2.** While they're reading, write the following questions on a sheet of newsprint and hang it where everyone can see it.

● What specifically did God promise to do for Abram?

● What, if anything, did Abram do to receive this promise?

● How would you describe Abram's behavior in Genesis 12:1-9? in Genesis 12:10–13:2?

● What were the results of Abram's actions in Genesis 12:1-9? in Genesis 12:10–13:2?

After groups finish reading, instruct them to spend the next 10 minutes discussing the questions on the newsprint. Have each group assign one person to record the group's responses and report them to the rest of the class.

After 10 minutes, ask group representatives to summarize their groups' conclusions. Then have the entire class discuss the following questions. Ask:

- How can we explain Abram benefiting from his deceit?

- What does this passage teach about God's commitment to his word? to us?

- How can knowing that God always keeps his promises help us overcome our fears?

Say: **God was so committed to Abram and his promise to him that he blessed Abram even when Abram seemed unworthy of it. In the same way,** ▷ **God keeps his promises to us even when we don't deserve it. Our security rests in God's faithfulness, not in our ability to earn God's favor. God has promised us certain things, and knowing that God will always keep those promises can help us deal with the fears that often plague us.**

Then have group members brainstorm biblical promises that address the specific fears they shared earlier. Have people write down any relevant promises next to the fears they listed on their papers. Encourage groups to identify at least one promise for each fear that was mentioned.

After five minutes, get everyone's attention and say: **We'll probably never be completely free from fear in this life, but we can learn how to overcome our fears. We know that** ▷ **God keeps his promises to us even when we don't deserve it. So, we can defeat our fears and insecurities by learning what God has promised to us and then trusting God to do exactly what he's said.**

T H E   P O I N T ▷

TEACHER TIP

T H E   P O I N T ▷

You can use the "What Has God *Really* Promised?" handout (p. 49) to help people match promises to their fears. Either write the biblical passages listed on the handout on newsprint or have people complete the handout and then apply what they've learned to their fears.

■■■■■■■■■■■■■■■■■■■■■■■■■■■■

FOR *Even Deeper* **DISCUSSION**

Form groups of four or fewer to discuss the following questions:

- When might fear be a healthy or positive emotion? To what extent should we attempt to overcome healthy fear? How can we balance faith in God with healthy fear?

- Did God sanction and bless Abram's deception or simply allow Abram to benefit from it? To what extent does God bless us through our wrongdoings? in spite of them?

■■■■■■■■■■■■■■■■■■■■■■■■■■■■

Apply·It·To·Life™ *This Week!*

The "Apply-It-To-Life This Week!" handout (p. 50) helps people further explore the issues uncovered in today's class. Give everyone a photocopy of the handout. Encourage class members to take time during the coming week to explore the questions and activities on the handout.

Help Our Unbelief
(up to 10 minutes)

Keep people in their foursomes. Have each group member identify one promise from God that he or she has a difficult time believing. After everyone has named a promise, have group members discuss the following questions. After each question, ask for volunteers to report their groups' responses. Ask:

- **Why do you think these promises are hard to believe?**

- **How can we increase our faith in God and his promises?**

Say: **Now silently answer this question: What will you do this week to increase your faith in God and his promises?** Pause. **We can trust God completely because ▷ God always keeps his promises, even when we don't deserve it. Let's close today's class by thanking God for his faithfulness and asking God to help us trust him more.**

◁ THE POINT

Have group members close in prayer, thanking God for always keeping his promises and asking God to help each other trust him to keep even those promises that are difficult to believe.

 ## For Extra Time

MORE PROMISES
(up to 15 minutes)

Before class, write down at least 10 biblical promises not listed on the "What Has God *Really* Promised?" handout (p. 49). For help locating promises, consult *The Bible Promise Book* (available in various English versions), *The Jesus Person Pocket Promise Book* by David Wilkerson, or some similar resource.

Form groups of four and assign two promises to each group. Instruct group members to answer the questions on the "What Has God *Really* Promised?" handout for each promise. After six minutes, ask groups to report what they've discovered. Then have the entire class discuss the following questions:

- **How have we neglected some of these promises?**
- **How have we misunderstood some of the promises?**
- **How can we better apply these promises to our lives?**

HISTORY REPEATS ITSELF
(up to 10 minutes)

Form groups of four. Assign half of the groups Genesis 20:1-18 (Abraham gives Sarah to Abimelech) and the other half Genesis 26:1-14 (Isaac gives Rebekah to Abimelech). Tell groups to compare their accounts with Genesis 12:10–13:2 by answering the following questions:

- How are the details of the accounts similar? different?
- How are the messages of the accounts similar? different?

After eight minutes, have groups briefly report their answers. Then ask the entire class:

- **What do these stories teach about God's commitment to his promises? about our responsibility to God? about our responsibility to others?**

WHAT HAS GOD REALLY PROMISED?

READ THE ASSIGNED biblical passage, then discuss the questions below. Write your insights in the space below the biblical reference. Repeat the process for each biblical passage you've been assigned. You have five minutes to discuss each biblical passage.

▶ What specifically does the biblical passage promise?

▶ What conditions, if any, are attached to the promise?

▶ To whom is the promise made? Does it still apply to us?

▶ What other biblical principles qualify or limit the promise?

▶ **MATTHEW 28:18-20**

▶ **2 CHRONICLES 7:11-16**

▶ **PROVERBS 3:9-10**

▶ **1 JOHN 1:9**

▶ **JAMES 5:14-16**

▶ **ISAIAH 40:28-31**

▶ **PHILIPPIANS 4:14-19**

▶ **PSALM 145:17-20**

Apply·It·To·Life™
This Week!

I Will Bless You

God keeps his promises to us even
when we don't deserve it.
Genesis 12:1–13:2

Reflecting on God's Word

Each day this week, read one of the following Scriptures and examine what it teaches about God and his promises. Then evaluate how well you are applying the message of the passage to your life. List your discoveries in the space under each passage.

Day 1: Lamentations 3:19-33. Judgment isn't God's final word to his people.

Day 2: 2 Timothy 2:11-13. God remains faithful even when we've been unfaithful.

Day 3: Psalm 36:5-12. God's steadfast love is available to any who seek it.

Day 4: Hebrews 10:35-39. Those who live by faith will receive God's promises.

Day 5: Exodus 34:1-10. God forgives his people so he can live among them.

Day 6: 1 Corinthians 10:1-14. God always provides a way for us to avoid sin.

Beyond Reflection

God selected Abram to be a blessing to all people (Genesis 12:1-3), and he expects no less of us (Matthew 5:43-47; 28:18-20; Galatians 6:10; James 1:27). At the end of each day, think about your interactions with others and record in a journal ways in which you were a blessing in someone's life. Also note situations in which you had a negative effect on someone and think of ways you can turn that negative interaction into something positive.

Coming Next Week: God Planned It for Good
(Genesis 39:1-23 and 50:15-21)

God Planned It for Good

God can transform human evil into his good.

◀ THE POINT

OBJECTIVES

Participants will
- discuss how God used past losses to accomplish something good,
- identify ways God is at work in the difficult situations of their lives, and
- discover how to respond to the good and evil circumstances of life.

BIBLE BASIS

Look up the Scriptures for this lesson. Then read the following background paragraphs to see how the passages relate to people today.

Genesis 39:1-23 describes Joseph's experiences as a slave and a prisoner in Egypt.

According to Genesis 37, Joseph knew that God had destined him to rule over his entire family. His open discussion of that fact, however, did little to promote family harmony. Rather, it increased and intensified the ill will that Joseph's older brothers already felt toward their father's favorite son. Eventually their hatred for Joseph grew so intense that they sold him into slavery and led their father to believe that he was dead.

Being estranged from his family and forcibly taken from his home were the first of many losses Joseph would endure before he enjoyed his promised rule. Genesis 39 describes three other losses Joseph had to face. As a house slave for the Egyptian official Potiphar, Joseph lost

GENESIS 39:1-23

his freedom and self-determination. It's true that God blessed Joseph in this situation, but that hardly altered his status. Joseph remained a piece of property owned by Potiphar. Then Joseph lost his reputation to a vicious lie. Potiphar's wife and Joseph knew that he was entirely innocent, but everyone else apparently believed that he was guilty of attempted rape. Consequently, Joseph was put in prison, where he lost what little freedom he had enjoyed in Potiphar's house.

Still, there were some things no human would ever be able to steal from Joseph. For example, Joseph maintained his integrity at all times. Joseph never used his losses as an excuse to complain or to compromise his commitment to God. Moreover, Joseph never lost God's presence. God was "with" Joseph when he served in Potiphar's house (39:2, 3) and when he served time in prison (39:21, 23). Finally, Joseph retained God's favor and success in every situation. In fact, God so favored Joseph that he became an agent of God's "blessing" to those around him (39:5).

We learn at least two things from Joseph's experiences. First, evil people and unfortunate situations may threaten our enjoyment of God's promises, but they will never prevent God from keeping his word. In addition, since God's promises often come under threat, we shouldn't allow threatening situations to shape our view of God or shake our faith in his goodness. Rather, we should follow Joseph's example of trusting God and maintaining integrity in every situation.

GENESIS 50:15-21

In Genesis 50:15-21, Joseph explained how God transformed his brothers' evil into something good.

After more than two years in prison, Joseph began to see his losses reversed and his dreams fulfilled. First, Joseph moved from the prison to the palace, where he became second only to Pharaoh in all of Egypt (41:41-43). Then, with God's assistance, Joseph saved many people—including his own family—from starvation during a severe famine (41:1–42:2; 47:13-26). In time, Joseph was even reunited with the members of his family (42:1–47:12), and eventually Joseph's older brothers bowed down to him, just as his dream had predicted (50:18, compare with 37:5-10).

After his father died, Joseph could have exploited his power and his brothers' weakness to punish his brothers for their crimes. Joseph, however, chose to pardon instead of to punish. In explaining himself, Joseph expressed the central theological truth of the book of Genesis: "You planned evil against me, but God planned it for good" (50:20a). Joseph had suffered all kinds of evil at the hands of humans, but in it all he saw the sovereign hand of God. Not only had God protected Joseph in the midst of his distress, God had also transformed the human evil that caused his distress into something undeniably good. In sum, God is so powerful and so good that even human evil cannot keep him from accomplishing his good will.

We can neither deny nor escape the pervasive presence of evil in the world. It touches Christians and non-Christians alike. We can, however, affirm the presence of God and his goodness even in the middle of an evil situation. We can overcome evil by trusting in the goodness of God in every circumstance. Use this lesson to help your class members trust God and his goodness even during the bad times they go through.

THIS LESSON AT A GLANCE

Section	Minutes	What Participants Will Do	Supplies
OPENING	up to 10	**MEMORABLE YEARS**—Discuss how good and bad experiences affected their relationship with God.	
BIBLE EXPLORATION AND APPLICATION	35 to 45	☐ Option 1: **LOSSES INTO GAINS**—Study Genesis 39:1-23 to discover how God turned Joseph's losses into gains and discuss how God can use their losses to accomplish good things.	Bibles, "Joseph's Loss, Everyone's Gain" handouts (p. 61), index cards, pencils
	25 to 35	☐ Option 2: **GOD WITH US**—Discuss times they felt God was or was not present, examine God's presence with Joseph in Genesis 39:1-23 and 50:15-21, and talk about God's active presence in their lives.	Bibles, paper, pencils, newsprint, marker, tape
CLOSING	up to 10	**APPROPRIATE RESPONSES**—Discuss and pray about how they should respond to God in the various situations of their lives.	Newsprint, marker, tape
FOR EXTRA TIME	up to 15	**HOW IS GOD WITH US?**—Examine selected biblical texts to discover the various forms God's presence takes.	Paper, pencils
	up to 5	**COURSE REFLECTION**—Describe what they've learned from this course.	

Memorable Years

(up to 10 minutes)

To begin class, tell people to form pairs. Have partners tell each other about the best year they've had.

Allow two minutes for discussion, then tell partners to describe their most difficult year. After several minutes, have pairs discuss the following questions. Ask:

- **What made the best year better than other years? What made the bad year so difficult?**

- **How did you feel about God during the good times? during the bad times?**

- **What did you think God's attitude toward you was during the good times? during the bad times?**

THE POINT▷

Say: **It's not unusual for our situations to affect not only our moods and attitudes but also our perceptions of God's relationship to us. It's especially easy to lose perspective when bad things happen to us, but our faith can survive the worst of times if we understand that ▷ God can transform human evil into his good.**

BIBLE EXPLORATION AND APPLICATION

☐ **OPTION 1:**

Losses Into Gains

(35 to 45 minutes)

Before class, make one photocopy of the "Joseph's Loss, Everyone's Gain" handout (p. 61) for each class member.

Give each person six index cards and a pencil. Tell everyone to write the three most painful losses they've experienced on three of the cards (one loss per card).

After several minutes, instruct people to form groups of four. Have group members each describe one of their losses to the rest of the group. Then have group members discuss the following questions. After each question, ask for volunteers to summarize their groups' responses for the rest of the class. Ask:

- **In what ways were our losses similar? In what ways were they different?**

- **What were the dominant emotions these losses evoked?**

TEACHER
TIP

Reliving the pain of these losses may arouse strong emotions. Encourage group members to be sensitive to and supportive of each other by allowing people to cry or even to choose not to talk about their past losses.

- **How did these losses affect your attitude about life?**

- **How did the losses affect your view of God? your relationship with God?**

Then instruct group members to write on the remaining cards the three most important persons or things in their lives (one per card). After everyone has finished writing, have each person hold up the three cards and take one card from the group member on his or her right. Then have group members discuss the following questions. Ask:

- **How would losing this person or thing change your day-to-day life?**

- **How do you think you'd react to losing this person or thing?**

- **How might this loss affect your attitude about life? your relationship with God?**

Have people retrieve and keep their cards for later use. Then say: **It's common for people who lose something important also to lose their perspective about God and his presence in their lives. We learn from the experiences of Joseph, however, that there's always more to the picture than the losses we may see.**

Give everyone a copy of the "Joseph's Loss, Everyone's Gain" handout. Tell people to work together with their group members to complete the handout.

After 10 minutes, ask groups to summarize their insights and answers for the rest of the class. Then have group members discuss the following questions. Ask:

- **How are the losses we discussed earlier similar to Joseph's losses? How are they different?**

- **What does this passage teach us about God's relationship to us during times of loss?**

- **What does this passage teach us about God's response to the losses we experience?**

Say: **One of the clear implications of this passage is that God transformed Joseph's losses into everyone's gain. Later in his life, Joseph expressed the same conviction to the very brothers who had sold him into slavery.** Read **Genesis 50:20** aloud. Say: **Joseph knew that**  **God can transform human evil into his good, so Joseph trusted in God's goodness even when life seemed bad.**

Instruct everyone to write on each of the three index cards that list his or her past losses one way God has used that loss to accomplish something good. Encourage anyone who can't think of a positive result to keep the card

TEACHER
TIP

Instead of having people randomly take cards from each other, you may want to tell people they must each choose to give up one of the three important things. Then have everyone hand that card to the group member on his or her left.

◄ THE POINT

and to ask God to reveal how the loss resulted in something good.

After several minutes, ask for volunteers to share with the entire class how God turned their past losses into gains. Then have group members help each other think of ways God could accomplish something good even through the loss of the most important things they listed earlier. Encourage everyone to list at least one idea on each of his or her three remaining cards.

After several minutes, say: **Although God has promised to do good things for and through us, he hasn't said that everything that happens will be good. In all likelihood, someday we'll have to face the loss of someone or something important to us. Therefore, we need to learn today that ▷ God can transform human evil into his good. No matter what happens to us, we'll never lose God's presence or his commitment to turn the bad things in our lives into something good.**

T H E   P O I N T ▷

■■■■■■■■■■■■■■■■■■■■■■■■■■■■■■

FOR *Even Deeper*
DISCUSSION

Form groups of four or fewer to discuss the following questions:

● Why do you think God allowed Joseph to experience loss? To what extent could God have accomplished the same things without Joseph suffering these losses? What does this imply about how God is involved in our lives when we experience losses?

● How did Joseph's faith in God's goodness affect his attitude? his actions? How should we respond to the evil things that happen to us?

■■■■■■■■■■■■■■■■■■■■■■■■■■■■■■

□ **O P T I O N   2 :**

God With Us

(25 to 35 minutes)

Have people form groups of four. Instruct group members each to describe one time they felt God's presence in their lives and one time they didn't feel God's presence. After everyone has shared, have group members discuss the following questions. After each question, ask for volunteers to report their groups' answers to the rest of the class. Ask:

● **What specific things led you to feel that God was present? that God was absent?**

- How was your perception of God's presence affected by your situation? by your spiritual condition?

- Looking back, how accurate was your assessment of God's presence or absence in your life?

Say: **Probably every person here wants to see and feel God's presence, but sometimes the situations of life make it difficult to do so. The story of Joseph has a message for those of us who want to know where God is and what God is doing when life is difficult.**

Give each group a sheet of paper and a pencil. Instruct groups to read **Genesis 39:1-23.** While they're reading, write the following instructions on a sheet of newsprint and hang it where everyone can see it.
- List everything positive about Joseph's situation.
- List everything negative about Joseph's situation.
- List every verse that mentions God's presence.
- List every result of God's presence with Joseph.

After groups finish reading, have each group appoint someone to record and report its answers. Tell groups they have five minutes to complete the instructions on the newsprint.

After five minutes, have representatives report their groups' insights to the rest of the class. Then have group members discuss the following questions. Ask:

- **How did Joseph's changing situation affect God's presence with him?**

- **In practical terms, how did God's presence benefit Joseph? those around Joseph?**

- **What do Joseph's experiences teach us about God's presence in our lives? about the results of God's presence?**

Have someone read **Genesis 50:15-21** aloud. Then say: **Joseph knew that God had been with him even during the hard times, so he could recognize how** ▶**God had transformed the bad things in his life into something incredibly good. As we grow in our knowledge of and faith in God's constant presence, we'll see God's goodness in action, too.**

Have group members each describe a situation in which they currently find it difficult to see God at work. For example, someone might describe the inability to find work or the apparent breakdown of a marriage. After everyone has shared, instruct group members to discuss the following questions. Encourage people to help each other see how God is or might be at work in each situation. Ask:

B I B L E INSIGHT

Just as God had promised in Genesis 12:1-3, he blessed other people through Abram and his descendants. Genesis 39:5 notes that God blessed everything Potiphar owned because of Joseph. God used the evil in Joseph's life to bless Potiphar, an Egyptian who probably worshiped the false gods of Egypt. Although Potiphar didn't deserve God's blessing, he received it because of his relationship with one of God's people.

◀ T H E   P O I N T

T E A C H E R TIP

This would be an excellent place to have groups discuss the first set of "For Even Deeper Discussion" questions provided at the end of this activity.

- **What specific evidences of God's presence can you see in this situation?**

- **How might God use this situation for the good of others? for your own good?**

- **How should knowing that God is always with you affect your attitude? your behavior?**

THE POINT ▷

Say: **Not everything that happens to us is good, but knowing that ▷ God can transform human evil into his good will enable us to trust God in every situation. When life becomes difficult, we need to remember that God is always with us and is committed to turning the evil that comes our way into something very good.**

BIBLE INSIGHT

God's promise to be "with" his people means different things at different times. Among other things, God's presence can signify divine approval or provide success, power, or protection (Genesis 26:3, 24; 28:15; 2 Samuel 7:3; Matthew 28:20; Acts 18:10). The one constant is God's identification with us. God doesn't always protect us from evil, but he always goes through the situation with us. God identifies himself so closely with us that he empathizes with us completely.

FOR *Even Deeper* DISCUSSION

Form groups of four or fewer to discuss the following questions:

- What does it mean that God is "with" the missionary suffering persecution? the Christian who just got a promotion? the child who is regularly beaten?

- In what sense is God with us when we sin? Is God with us in different ways at different times? Explain. How might our behavior affect God's presence with us? our perception of God's presence?

Apply·It·To·Life™
This Week!

The "Apply-It-To-Life This Week!" handout (p. 62) helps people further explore the issues uncovered in today's class. Give everyone a photocopy of the handout. Encourage class members to take time during the coming week to explore the questions and activities on the handout.

CLOSING

Appropriate Responses
(up to 10 minutes)

Keep people in groups of four. Write the words "promise," "threat," and "blessing" across the top of a sheet of newsprint and hang it where everyone can see it.

Say: **In our last study, we learned that God always keeps his promises, even when we may not deserve it. But, as we discovered today, that doesn't mean that God gives us what he's promised right away. More often than not, we have to face some sort of threat to God's promise before we enjoy the blessing of God's faithfulness. Often, ▷ God keeps his promise to bless us by turning some human evil into his good. Recognizing this progression from promise to threat to blessing helps us understand how we should respond to God in every situation.**

◁ T H E   P O I N T

For example, if we don't know what God has promised us, we probably need to search until we discover what God has and has not promised. On the newsprint, write "search" under "promise." **When life threatens what we know God has promised, we need to trust that God will do exactly what he's said.** Write "trust" under "threat." **Finally, when we're experiencing God's blessing, we should thankfully enjoy God's faithfulness to his word.** Write "thank and enjoy" underneath "blessing."

Instruct group members each to name one area of their lives in which they want to know what God has promised. Then have someone in each group pray that God would reveal his specific promises for those areas. After groups finish praying, tell group members each to name one area of their lives in which they see God's promise being threatened and have someone else in the group pray for those needs. Then instruct group members each to name one area in which they're currently enjoying God blessing and have someone in the group thank God for those blessings.

After groups have finished praying, close in prayer, thanking God for his goodness and faithfulness to his promises in the face of every threat.

Thank each person specifically for his or her contribution to the course.

Ask people what they liked most about the course and what parts they'd like to see changed. If possible, have people complete the "Course Reflection" in the For Extra Time section. Please note class members' comments (along with your own) and send them to Adult Curriculum Editor, Group Publishing, Inc., Dept. BK, Box 481, Loveland, CO 80539. We want your feedback so we can make each course we publish better than the last. Thanks!

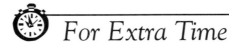 *For Extra Time*

HOW IS GOD WITH US?

(up to 15 minutes)

Form groups of four and give each group a sheet of paper and a pencil. Assign each group two of the following passages: Genesis 26:3, 24; 28:15; Joshua 1:5-9; 2 Samuel 7:3; Isaiah 41:10; Matthew 28:20; Acts 18:10; Philippians 4:8-9. Instruct groups to read their passages and list the various forms that God's presence with his people takes. After 10 minutes, have groups report what they've discovered. Then ask the entire class the following questions:

- **What forms has God's presence taken in your life?**

- **How can you become more aware of God's presence?**

COURSE REFLECTION

(up to 5 minutes)

Ask people to reflect on the past four lessons. Then have them take turns completing the following sentences:

- Something I learned in this course was...
- If I could tell friends about this course, I'd say...
- Something I'll do differently because of this course is...

Please note class members' comments (along with your own) and send them to Adult Curriculum Editor, Group Publishing, Inc., Dept. BK, Box 481, Loveland, CO 80539. We want your feedback so we can make each course we publish better than the last. Thanks!

Joseph's Loss ⬇ ⬆ EVERYONE'S Gain

Work with your group members to complete this handout. You have 10 minutes to complete all the instructions.

1. Read the information in the FYI box and Genesis 39:1-23.

2. Based on what you've read, list everything that Joseph lost in the "Losses" column below.

3. Now list everything that Joseph gained or retained in the "Gains" column.

4. Discuss the questions below.

> **F.Y.I.**
>
> According to Genesis 37, Joseph knew that God had destined him to rule over his entire family. His open discussion of that fact, however, did little to promote family harmony. Rather, it increased and intensified the ill will that Joseph's older brothers already felt toward their father's favorite son. Eventually their hatred for Joseph grew so intense that they sold him into slavery and led their father to believe that he was dead.

Losses	Gains
_____	_____
_____	_____
_____	_____
_____	_____
_____	_____
_____	_____
_____	_____
_____	_____

DISCUSSION QUESTIONS:

● How did Joseph's losses affect his relationships with those around him? his relationship with God?

● How did God use Joseph's losses to benefit others? to benefit Joseph?

● To what extent was Joseph aware of what God was doing in his life?

Apply·It·To·Life™
This Week!

God Planned It for Good

God can transform human evil into his good.
Genesis 39:1-23 and 50:15-21

Reflecting on God's Word

Each day this week, read one of the following Scriptures and examine what it teaches about God's goodness. Then evaluate how well you are applying the message of the passage to your life. List your discoveries in the space under each passage.

Day 1: Psalm 145:8-16. God has compassion on all of creation.

Day 2: Acts 14:14-18. God sends good things to all people.

Day 3: Psalm 86:1-7. God answers the cries of his people.

Day 4: Ecclesiastes 5:18-20. God enables people to enjoy life.

Day 5: Psalm 34:6-18. God delivers his people from their troubles.

Day 6: Ezekiel 18:21-23. God is pleased when evil people repent.

Beyond Reflection

Become an agent of God's goodness to the people around you. Begin each day by asking God to give you at least one opportunity to do something good. Throughout the day, be attentive to the various opportunities God gives you and show God's goodness whenever you can. At the end of each day, thank God for extending his goodness to you and for allowing you to extend it to others.

Fellowship and Outreach Specials

Use the following activities any time you want. You can use them as part of (or in place of) your regular class activities, or you might consider planning a special event based on one or more of the ideas.

Ruling Responsibly

Set aside a Saturday to clean or tidy up some area within your church neighborhood. For example, you might want to pick up trash and pull weeds along the streets and sidewalks near your church. Or you could clean, repair, or refurbish the equipment and facilities at a local park or playground. Be sure to get permission from the proper authorities before performing any service beyond basic cleaning. If anyone asks why you want to make your neighborhood look better, explain that you're obeying God's commission to rule his creation responsibly (Genesis 1:26-28; 2:15).

Even Deeper

Study some of the events narrated in Genesis in greater depth. After the completion of the course, meet once a month to view and discuss one of the following videos from Group Publishing, Inc.
- *Noah's Ark: Fact or Fable?*
- *Noah's Ark: Was There a Worldwide Flood?*
- *Noah's Ark: What Happened to It?*
- *Sodom and Gomorrah: Legend or Real Event?*
- *Tower of Babel: Fact or Fiction?*

Each video comes with a discussion guide to help you focus on the important truths taught by each biblical event.

Other Views

Invite members of the community to a public forum at which different views about the origin of the world will be presented in a nonthreatening environment. For example, you might invite speakers who represent each of the following groups: those who believe the world is entirely the product of evolutionary processes, those who believe God used evolutionary processes to create the world, and those who believe the creation of the world was a direct act of God. After speakers present their views, allow people from the audience the opportunity to ask questions.

Encourage participants and observers to treat each other with kindness and respect, seeking only to understand (and not to refute) people with whom they disagree. At some point in the forum, discuss how each perspective might influence one's view of God, humanity, and the world. To conclude the forum, thank people for participating and invite them to visit your class or church to learn more about God and his goodness.

Apply-It-To-Life™ Together

Create a meeting based on the "Apply-It-To-Life This Week!" handouts from the course. As a part of the meeting, ask volunteers to share what they discovered through each of the handouts. During the meeting, have people choose at least two "Beyond Reflection" activities to complete together. Establish a schedule for the completion of each of the activities they select.

Enjoying God's Good Food

Invite the members of your church to a potluck dinner or picnic at which everyone brings his or her favorite food or drink. To ensure that the meal is reasonably balanced, have people sign up for categories such as salad, main dish, dessert, and drink. When people finish eating, ask them to share specific ways God has shown his goodness to them during the past year. Close by singing "God Is So Good" or some other song that celebrates God's goodness.